KALI'S TRAVELS

MARLENE NORGARD

Copyright © 2024 Marlene Norgard
Second Edition

All rights reserved. No part of this book may be reproduced or transmitted in any form or by any means, electronic or mechanical, including photocopying, recording or by any information storage and retrieval system, without written permission from the author, except for brief quotations as would be used in a review.

ISBN 978-1-962729-02-4 (Paperback)

Published in the United States by Inspire
An Adducent Creative Imprint
Adducent, Inc.
Jacksonville, Florida

To my baby girl Kali, you are the most precious gift and I have learned so much because of you. You have made me look through the eyes of a child to help understand things as children see them.

My hopes for you as you grow is that you continue to thrive, accomplish, and be thankful for the people and love around you wherever life may take you. I love you.

—Mommy

I was born in Hawaii, a very special place of aloha (love). It has big blue sparkling water, delicious poke bowls, and friendly *kama 'aina* (local people) all around.

I asked Mommy, "Can we stay here, I really like it here?"

Mommy replied, "No we cannot, sweetheart. When we are needed we have to move. But do not worry, Kali. Hawaii will always be in your heart."

A little time later Mommy told me that we were needed and had to move.

"Where do we have to go, Mommy?" I asked.

Mommy replied, "Camp Butler, Okinawa, my dear."

The movers arrived to pack all my things in my room. I was sad to see everything go into a box. I didn't know if I would see it again. There were so many boxes piled up to the ceiling, but Mommy told me we would see it soon in our new home. I said good-bye to the big blue sparkly ocean, the delicious poke bowls, and the friendly *kama 'aina*.

We arrived in Okinawa, and my tummy was so nervous.

"How will I meet new friends, Mommy?"

She told me it will happen, I just need to wait. A few days later I met Greyson, and we had so much fun together. He showed me so many fun things to do in Okinawa.

Greyson and his mommy took me to the Churaumi Aquarium to see sting rays as big as cars! We slid down slides with fast rollers two stories high, and he shared my big bowl of ramen with me. He showed me how wonderful Okinawa can be. I met a good friend just as my mommy said.

Greyson and I always went out together. We went to the Tug of War in Naha, where they have a big, BIG rope in the streets. We each took a piece of the rope home with us. It is a very old tradition. We explored the thick jungles and the white sand beaches. He was my best friend.

A few years later Mommy told me we were needed somewhere else. We had to move to another home.

"Where are we needed?" I asked.

"Camp Pendleton, California," she replied.

I liked it here, and I really liked my friend. I asked if we could stay here in Okinawa.

Mommy told me, "Do not worry, Kali, Okinawa will always be in your heart and Greyson will always be your friend."

The movers came once more, and I said good-bye to the Churaumi Aquarium; the two-story roller slides; the white sand beaches; the big, BIG rope; and to my friend Greyson.

I watched the boxes get packed up again. Each one had a special number on a piece of blue tape. I made sure to memorize my numbers on my boxes to make sure I got it back. Off to Camp Pendleton we went on a very large plane.

Mommy showed me our new house and let me pick my room. Of course, I picked the big one. Mommy said I can decorate it however I wanted, so I told Mommy I loved birds and Hawaii. So she got me a lot of birds to hang around the room. It looked like they were flying! She also got me a lei, Hawaiian books, and starfish to make it look like the Hawaiian sea. I loved my new room.

After we unpacked our boxes, we went to a playground and I met Dominic. He was really nice and showed me all the wonderful things to do in California. We went to Disneyland to go see our favorite characters and Knott's Berry Farm, California's very first theme park. And for lunch we had the most delicious burritos. I made a wonderful new friend named Dominic.

A few years later Mommy told me we were needed somewhere else. I asked her where, and she replied, "Camp Lejeune, North Carolina."

I like it here in California, and I really liked my friend Dominic. I wanted to stay.

Mommy said, "Do not worry, Kali, California will always be in your heart and Dominic will always be your friend."

"Okay, Mommy," I said.

The boxes were packed up all over again, and off we went to Camp Lejeune, North Carolina. We drove in a car this time. We were able to see so many interesting things traveling across the country. I said good-bye to Disneyland with our favorite characters, good-bye to California's first theme park, and good-bye to those yummy burritos, and my friend Dominic.

I stood in front of our new home. It was a blue house on a quiet road with a big backyard and a big wide road to play on. Mommy let me pick my room again and decorate it. I was feeling alone, but it would not be for long.

I met Ava. She lived down the street, and she was very kind. She showed me all the beautiful things about North Carolina. We went hunting for shark's teeth on Onslow beach, we saw a living shipwreck at the North Carolina Aquarium at Pine Knoll Shores, and we shared the tastiest barbeque.

Ava was my best friend. I looked at my mommy and asked her, "Mommy, are we needed somewhere else soon?"

She told me, "We will soon, baby girl. But do not worry, Kali, North Carolina will always be in your heart and Ava will always be your friend."

Pretty soon the time came that we had to move, and I started feeling lonely. Mommy came into the house and handed me some pieces of paper. They were pictures and letters from all my friends. Greyson, Dominic, and Ava had all sent me something to remember our memories together. My heart felt happy. Mommy was right. They were always in my heart.

About the Author

Born and raised in New Jersey in a small country town full of horses, farms, wide open fields, and mountains as our backdrop, I never imagined how much bigger my world would become.

I got my Bachelor's Degree in Criminal Justice and Associate of Science Degree in Crime Scene Technology and worked as a crime scene technician. I married the love of my life as he entered the US Marine Corps. Now, I'm a military spouse and a mother of two beautiful children. And I found my niche in writing.

Experiencing the many outlooks, challenges, and hardships of military life and seeing not only my children but also my friends' children struggle with specific issues within that life, I have made it my mission to write about those issues and open a dialogue for conversations about them. I am the author of the children's books *Daddy's Deploying, Kali's Travels,* and *My Star-Spangled Friend*. This series means a lot to me. I thank my son Deklan and daughter Kali for their compassion and understanding. They entrusted me with their feelings I could use to write these books that I hope will help connect you with your child to show them that others feel just the same. It's okay to feel as they do and to know we can do something about it. We can talk, share, and make sure they feel safe and loved wherever they are.

www.MarlenesMilitaryKids.com

www.ingramcontent.com/pod-product-compliance
Lightning Source LLC
Chambersburg PA
CBHW041433040426
42451CB00021B/3493